CODE MONKEYS

Use Technology

BY JOHN WOOD

CRABTREE
PUBLISHING COMPANY
WWW.CRABTREEBOOKS.COM

CRABTREE
PUBLISHING COMPANY
WWW.CRABTREEBOOKS.COM

Author: John Wood

Editorial Director: Kathy Middleton

Editors: Robin Twiddy, Janine Deschenes

Proofreader: Melissa Boyce, Petrice Custance

Designed by: Danielle Webster-Jones

**Production coordinator and
  Prepress technician:** Margaret Amy Salter

Print coordinator: Katherine Berti

Images are courtesy of Shutterstock.com. With thanks to Getty Images, Thinkstock Photo and iStockphoto. Cover & throughout - Ori Artiste. 2 - Ann679. 4 - Ann679, GoodStudio, SK Design, feelplus. 5 - EmBaSy. 6 - Oleksiy Mark. 7 - No-Te Eksarunchai, charles taylor, Tarikdiz. 8 - Lemberg Vector studio. 9 - Macrovector, hanss, Vector Up. 10-11 - Abscent. 14 - iunewind, grmarc. 15 - Nikola Stanisic, Phil's Mommy, I000s_ pixels, sezer66. 16 - tynyuk, grebeshkovmaxim. 17 - Be.sign. 18 - 0beron. 19 - Sue Tansirimas. 20 - elenabsl. 21 - metamorworks, Beatriz Gascon J. 22 - NeuendorfNiclas, Iurii Kiliian, mei yanotai, Andrew Rybalko, Andrei Kuzmik. 23 - vladwel.
Additional illustration by Danielle Webster-Jones.

Scratch is a project of the Scratch Foundation, in collaboration with the Lifelong Kindergarten Group at the MIT Media Lab. It is available for free at https://scratch.mit.edu

Library and Achives Canada Cataloguing in Publication

Title: Code monkeys use technology / by John Wood.
Other titles: Using technology
Names: Wood, John, 1990- author.
Series: Code monkeys.
Description: Series statement: Code monkeys | Originally published under title: Using technology. King's Lynn: BookLife, 2020. | Includes index.
Identifiers: Canadiana (print) 20200222635 | Canadiana (ebook) 20200222724 |
  ISBN 9780778781516 (hardcover) |
  ISBN 9780778781554 (softcover) |
  ISBN 9781427125859 (HTML)
Subjects: LCSH: Computer science—Juvenile literature. | LCSH: Computer programming—Juvenile literature.
Classification: LCC QA76.23 .W66 2021 | DDC j004—dc23

Library of Congress Cataloging-in-Publication Data

Names: Wood, John, 1990- author.
Title: Code monkeys use technology / by John Wood.
Description: New York : Crabtree Publishing Company, 2021. |
  Series: Code monkeys | Includes index.
Identifiers: LCCN 2020016162 (print) | LCCN 2020016163 (ebook) |
  ISBN 9780778781516 (hardcover) |
  ISBN 9780778781554 (paperback) |
  ISBN 9781427125859 (ebook)
Subjects: LCSH: Computers--Juvenile literature. | Machine-to-machine communications--Juvenile literature.
Classification: LCC QA76.23 .W658 2021 (print) | LCC QA76.23 (ebook) |
  DDC 004--dc23
LC record available at https://lccn.loc.gov/2020016162
LC ebook record available at https://lccn.loc.gov/2020016163

Crabtree Publishing Company

www.crabtreebooks.com   1-800-387-7650
Published by Crabtree Publishing Company in 2021

©2020 BookLife Publishing Ltd.

Printed in the U.S.A./082020/CG20200601

**Published in Canada
Crabtree Publishing**
616 Welland Avenue
St. Catharines, Ontario
L2M 5V6

**Published in the United States
Crabtree Publishing**
347 Fifth Ave
Suite 1402-145
New York, NY 10016

Contents

Words with lines underneath, like this, can be found in the glossary on page 24.

Welcome
TO THE JUNGLE

Code monkeys are silly and smart. They want to learn all about computers and coding. You can follow the code monkeys and learn about coding too!

A code monkey's curiosity can get it into trouble. No! Bad code monkey! Bring back those wires!

SOME WORDS TO KNOW

COMPUTER

A machine that can carry out <u>instructions</u>.

CODING

Writing a set of instructions that tell computers what to do. The instructions are called code.

PROGRAMMER

A person who writes code, or puts instructions into a computer.

Computers are everywhere. Desktops, laptops, smartphones, and tablets are all computers. There are even computers in surprising places, from farm machines to classroom whiteboards.

Coding
IN THE WILD

Have you ever wondered how smart TVs know how to do things such as recommending movies or responding to voice commands? Smart TVs can do these tasks and more because programmers told them how!

Programmers write code that tells smart TVs how to do certain things. They write code to make other <u>devices</u>, such as toys, microwaves, and the computers in cars, work too!

Inputs AND Outputs

A computer is made up of many different parts. Some parts take in information. They are called input devices. Your keyboard is an input device. It makes sure the computer receives the letters you type. Other parts, called output devices, give out information. The computer screen is an output device. It makes sure you can see what's happening on the computer.

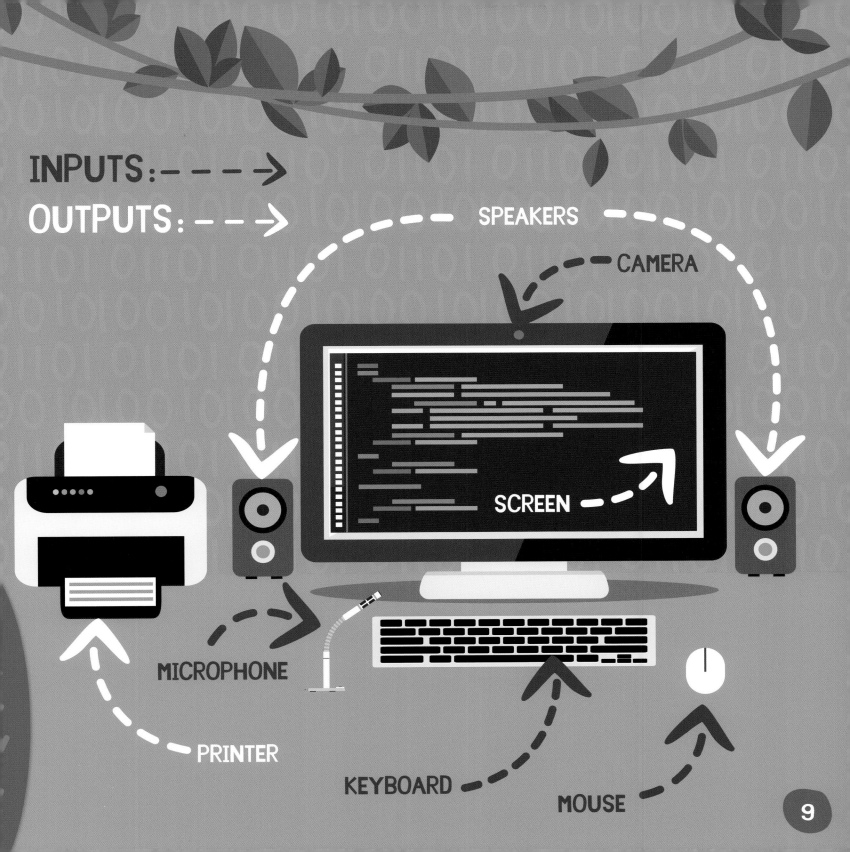

INPUTS: - - - →
OUTPUTS: - - →

SPEAKERS

CAMERA

SCREEN

MICROPHONE

PRINTER

KEYBOARD

MOUSE

9

Hardware AND Software

A computer's parts can be sorted into two groups: hardware and software.

Hardware is the parts you can touch. Examples of hardware are the keyboard and mouse. You can find a lot of hardware inside a computer too. Look for examples on these pages.

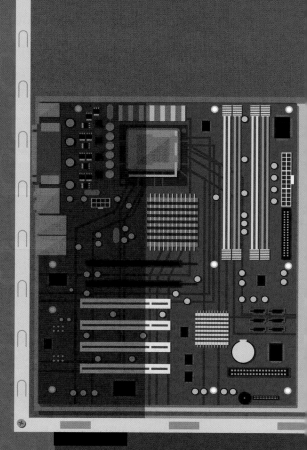

FAN
Fans keep the computer from getting too warm.

The parts of a computer that you cannot touch are called software. One example is an <u>application</u>, or app, on a smartphone. Software is built from code.

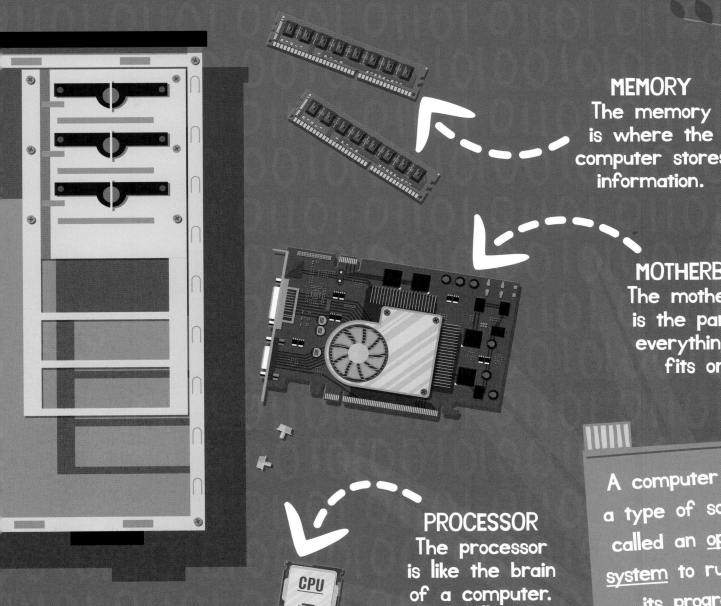

MEMORY
The memory is where the computer stores information.

MOTHERBOARD
The motherboard is the part that everything else fits onto.

PROCESSOR
The processor is like the brain of a computer. It follows instructions.

A computer needs a type of software called an <u>operating system</u> to run all of its <u>programs</u>.

Ones AND Zeroes

Computers use a language called binary to understand instructions. Binary is made out of ones and zeroes. Each letter in the English language is represented by a group of binary numbers.

This code monkey must use the binary language to <u>communicate</u> with the robot.

01101111
01101111
01101000

01101111
01101111
01101000

01100001
01101000

01100001
01101000

ooh ooh ah ah

12

Look below to learn some numbers and letters in binary.

Counting in binary

1 = 1
2 = 10
3 = 11
4 = 100
5 = 101

Letters in binary

A = 01000001
B = 01000010
C = 01000011
D = 01000100
E = 01000101

You can check online to learn many more letters and numbers in binary!

Turn the page to find out how programmers write code. →

TALKING IN Code

Binary can be difficult to understand. So programmers write code in special languages called programming languages. These languages are easier for humans to understand. Then this language is translated, or turned into, binary so the computer can understand the instructions.

Each programming language has different rules about how the code is written. Each language also uses different words and <u>symbols</u>.

There are many different programming languages. Certain programming languages are often used to write certain kinds of code.

HTML, CSS, and JavaScript are great for making websites.

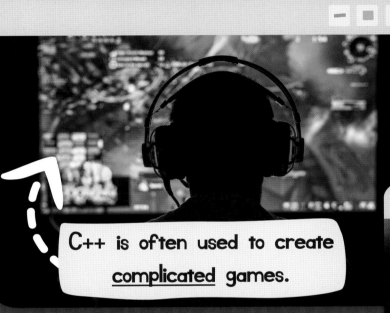

C++ is often used to create <u>complicated</u> games.

Python is a good programming language for building apps. It is made to be easy to use.

Scratch works well for people who are learning how to code. It uses simple blocks of instructions that users can easily put together.

SAFE MonkeYs

It is important to stay safe when you use the Internet. You can stay safe by not posting or telling others personal information. This includes your full name, where you live, or your phone number.

Instead of posting a picture of yourself online, it can be a good idea to use an <u>avatar</u> or a picture of your pet!

If you like to chat with friends online, make sure you talk only to people you know in person.

Another way to stay safe is to keep your passwords secret. A password is a mix of letters, numbers, and symbols that gives only you access to a program or a website. A password should be easy for you to remember, but hard for other people to guess.

Don't write your passwords down. Make sure you can remember them!

Climb TO SAFETY

We can use the Internet in so many ways. However, it can be confusing sometimes. You might see things you don't like or understand. You can stay safe by talking to a trusted adult about which websites are good to visit.

Do you have Internet rules at home or at school? They are in place to keep you and others safe. It is important to follow them!

If you see something that upsets or confuses you, leave the computer or put down the device. Talk to a trusted adult about what you saw.

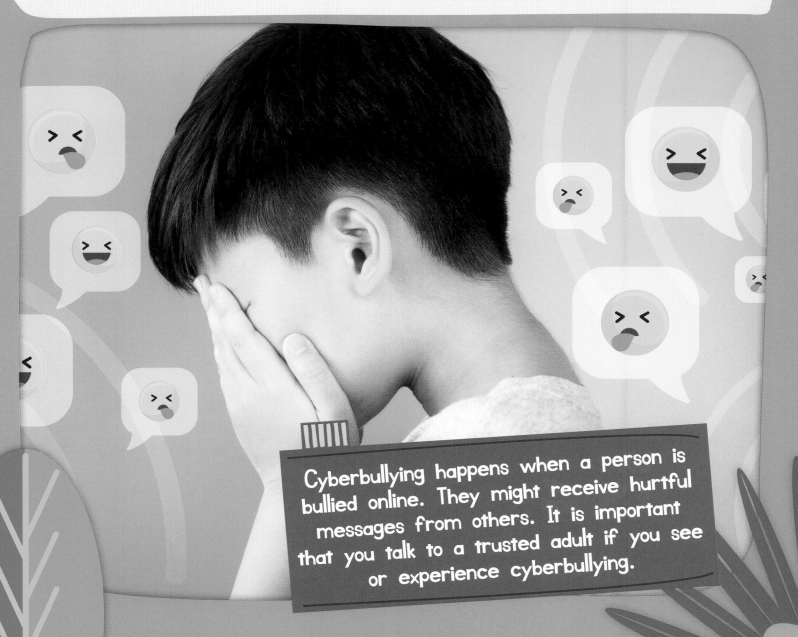

Cyberbullying happens when a person is bullied online. They might receive hurtful messages from others. It is important that you talk to a trusted adult if you see or experience cyberbullying.

Monkey See

In the future, the machines and devices around us will become more connected by computers and the Internet. One day, our fridges, laptops, cars, phones, and even coffee machines could all communicate with each other.

How do you imagine that computers and the Internet will change life in the future?

One example is self-driving cars. People are already working hard to create these cars. The cars communicate with each other so they can drive safely on the road.

One day, your smart fridge could send a message to your phone, telling you to order food that has run out.

MORE FOOD!

Monkey Do

It is time to practice your Internet safety skills. Can you come up with a list of tips to stay safe while using the Internet? Try to write down three to five tips. Share your list with a sibling, friend, or classmate.

1.

2.

3.

Code monkeys always have the best passwords! Now it is your turn. Try to come up with the perfect password. Include uppercase and lowercase letters. Include numbers and symbols, too. Your password shouldn't be easy for others to guess.

5JUMPingB@n@n@s!

Any passwords that include your personal information, such as your name, are easy for others to guess!

Glossary

application   A computer program that serves a specific purpose, such as an Internet browser

avatar   In computers, an illustration of a character that represents, or stands for, a person

communicate   To pass information between two or more people or devices

complicated   Made of many different parts and difficult to understand

devices   Machines or pieces of equipment designed to complete certain tasks

information   Numbers and facts that tell humans and computers about the world and the things in it

instructions   A set of steps that explain how something is done

operating system   A software program on a computer that turns instructions into binary language that the computer can understand

programs   Collections of instructions that let computers complete certain tasks

sibling   A brother or sister

symbols   Objects or pictures that represent, or stand for, something else

Index